Anxiety
ELEPHANTS

**A 31-DAY DEVOTIONAL
TO HELP STOMP OUT
YOUR ANXIETY**

CARIS SNIDER

BROOKSTONE
PUBLISHING GROUP

Anxiety Elephants:
A 31-Day Devotional to Help Stomp Out Anxiety
Caris Snider

Brookstone Publishing Group
P.O. Box 211, Evington, VA 24550
BrookstoneCreativeGroup.com

Ordering Information:
Special discounts are available on quantity purchases by corporations,
associations, and others. For details, contact
Brookstone Publishing Group at the address above.

ISBN: 978-1-949856-19-4 (print), 978-1-949856-20-0 (epub)

Introduction

The rumbling...do you hear it? Can you feel it? You are standing in the grocery store, or heading to the movies, or just about to sit down in church, and here they come—the Anxiety Elephants.

This is about the closest thing I can use to describe the sensation of an anxiety attack. You know the feeling, right? You are minding your own business and enjoying your day, meanwhile, the sneak attack is put into motion. Quiet at first—you hear and detect nothing. They lurk in the bushes waiting for the right moment to strike. At this point, it is too late. There is nothing you can do to stop them. Suddenly, they pounce—a herd of elephants jumps up and down on your chest. The party is going strong for them, but a party is not the way you would describe your own experience. It feels more like you're being pinned down, gripped in fear, and unable to move. One. Tiny. Inch.

If you struggle with what I've just described, know you are not alone.

Several years ago, I was in a place in my own life where anxiety paralyzed me. Until my first attack, I did not believe anxiety was a real thing. When people said they dealt with anxiety and needed prayer, I did not respond with the compassion of Jesus. I told them they needed to stop whining and complaining. I even said, "Just pray harder and trust God more." I had no idea about the depth of what they were experiencing—until one day, that all changed.

I hid my struggle against anxiety with an always smiling face. I was terrified people might find out. I thought Anxiety Elephants, as I like to call them, only came after me. I didn't know there were others who struggled with the same thing, who also desperately wanted to stomp out the beasts crushing the life out of them.

Over the next thirty-one days, I want to help you begin to stomp out your own Anxiety Elephants. As we journey, you will find scripture, tools, and action steps that were helpful for me—some will be repeated, but with a different approach, so you are fully equipped for victory. I believe they will be helpful for you, as well.

Think of this quest like a road trip. As you drive, you see signs telling you how many miles you have left to get to your destination. The signs are the same in color, shape, size, and location, the only difference between them is the number display, showing how many miles you have left. These reminders are given to you, so you know you are going the right way and feel encouraged to stay the course.

The Bible uses this same tactic of providing us with reminders. Throughout scripture, God used different people to deliver the same message—redemption, forgiveness, provision, and love.

Anxiety also uses repetition, but instead of offering hope, peace, and healing like God's Word, it attacks. And anxiety doesn't use a million contrasting messages to invade your life—the deceptions are always the same, just given with a slight variation in tone. In the following pages, we'll review some of those specific lies, but more so, you will find reminders to help you fight back when Anxiety Elephants attack. Truth must be repeated to break the hold of untruths looping in your mind—the Anxiety Elephant's favorite weapon. But as I've learned, we do not have to fall victim.

Now, are you ready to stomp? Let's go!

Day One

Come to me, all who are weary and burdened,
and I will give you rest. Take my yoke upon you
and learn from me, for I am gentle and humble
in heart, and you will find rest for your souls.

MATTHEW 11:28-29

Anxiety Elephants—where in the world do they come from?

Several years ago, I reached a place where anxiety debilitated me.
Previous to that experience, I had no idea what anxiety was or
what it felt like. For years, I'd worn a mask of perfection and convinced myself this "anxiety stuff" others talked about wasn't real.
Surely, people were simply feeling sorry for themselves, being lazy,
and simply not trusting God enough. Back then, if you'd told me
you dealt with anxiety and needed prayer, instead of receiving the
compassion of Jesus from me, I would have acted more like a high
school football coach pushing his team to play harder against a
winning opponent. I would have thought, and depending on how
deep our relationship went, maybe even said, "Stop your whining," or "Suck it up butter cup," and even, "You need to read your

Bible and pray more." I didn't yet comprehend the depths of pain and agony that anxiety-ridden people experience. In a single day, I found myself feeling smothered. It was as if someone had thrown me into a dark pit, and though I desperately wanted to get out, there was no light to help me see the way. I was undergoing my first anxiety attack.

The rumbling in my ears came first. It sounded like a helicopter blade going around and around—without stopping. My heart was beating like it never had before. For hours, the heaviest feeling I had ever experienced weighted me down. It left me breathless and I felt lifeless when it was over.

Close your eyes and imagine a herd of elephants running towards you as fast as they can. Picture them jumping on top of your chest like a trampoline, and they just—won't—stop. This is what an anxiety attack feels like! Sometimes, you can identify what blind-sided you, and sometimes, you have no idea what triggered the onset. But either way, while trapped beneath, all you want to do is escape.

From the start, I hid my anxiety behind a smile, terrified people would see my weakness and vulnerability. I didn't know there were others struggling with Anxiety Elephants. I've since discovered almost 300 million of us search for the light that will lead us out of that pit. We need a new way to live life.

For those of you joining me for the next thirty-one days, know it is for victory you turned the page and are reading day one. You may have even had an anxiety attack as you searched in a store or online, looking for something to help you. I remember those moments. Finding relief was a huge desire of my heart, but admitting I needed it was the biggest blockade for me to break through.

You've put cracks in the wall you've built up and reinforced for so long, simply by turning a page. This is a great start. As you continue, you will learn some things you didn't know about the causes of anxiety. There are actual triggers signaling those Anxiety Elephants to show up, but I will teach you how to stomp them out and overcome them. Each day's devotional will be filled with a scripture and encouraging story—reminders you aren't alone. Action steps, prayers, and an opportunity to journal will be awaiting you as you deal with each new day. At times, you will find these easy to accomplish, but some moments will stretch you. You will have to face your Anxiety Elephants head-on, but you will be equipped for the battle. You can go through this devotional as many times as you need, for ongoing support in your long-term success.

No matter what you do, you may still have moments where the breath is knocked out of you as the Anxiety Elephants kick you into a cloud of dirt and make you feel like you're landing on a hard, cold ground—I do. The difference is, now you will have the weapons to get up, fight back, and trample Anxiety Elephants when they do come. As the pages turn in this book, so do the moments in your life—change is happening. A shift is coming for you. Can you feel it?

Action Step

The very first thing I had to do when facing my anxiety was confess and pray. I had tried to hide it from everyone, including myself and God. It was time to stop. I encourage you, don't wait, confess and pray today. There is no shame or condemnation in Him, so trust He is listening and He cares about you. God wants you to have these weapons for overcoming Anxiety Elephants.

Prayer

Dear God, I have decided to no longer hide from you. I am tired of these Anxiety Elephants jumping on me and I am ready to fight back. Please forgive me for trying to do this on my own. I need You. I need the tools You have available for me to overcome. Amen.

Journal Your Thoughts Below

_____

_____

_____

_____

_____

_____

_____

_____

_____

_____

_____

_____

_____

_____

_____

_____

_____

_____

Day Two

The LORD is close to the brokenhearted and
saves those who are crushed in spirit.

PSALM 34:18

The constant pounding.

The constant berating.

The constant attacks.

The constant stomping.

It is a crushing feeling. Anxiety Elephants sneak in undetected. Immediately, punching. Beating. Verbally attacking you. This is their mission. You might look like you are standing tall on the outside, but you are crushed into a million different pieces on the inside.

While all of this is happening, no one else knows. People cannot hear the cries you withhold. They don't see the pain and emotional bruises you cover. You believe no one feels what you feel. "You are alone," Anxiety Elephants spew out as they pummel your mind. They hope to convince you no one cares. Is there anyone out there who really understands what you are going through?

At my lowest point, today's verse cracked the dam around my soul open. When I first read it, a river of tears rushed over the walls I had carefully constructed. No amount of waterproof mascara would have helped. I wept, because it felt as if God reached down and held my face between His two gentle hands. He lifted my chin from the downward position it had been in for years. He drew near to me, and through Psalm 34:18 said, "I'm here and I love you."

I'd like you to close your eyes and imagine God is sitting beside you right now, doing the same for you. Let God's tender words remove any shame or embarrassment you might feel.

When I went through this exercise, God let me know He was with me and He loved me. He had not given up on me—and God has not given up on you. Our Abba Father knows how to break through the rough exterior we have built up. He wants to permeate the broken places in your heart in a way only He can.

God has more for you. He will show you this gift of grace as you journey out from under the Anxiety Elephants. He no longer wants you to be in a place where you experience pain alone. Jesus came for the sick and hurting which means you and me. He is near. Open up to Him today.

Action Step

Close your eyes, sit or kneel in a place where you feel comfortable. Experience God's loving embrace. Allow His presence to enter into those broken places in your heart, the ones you are convinced can never be healed. Open your soul and give His love a chance to restore your hope. Your Good, Good Father wants to be the lifter of your head. He is cupping your face in His hands right now and He is saying, "I love you."

Prayer

Father, I need your love today. I am asking you to pull me close to you. Lift my head and wipe away my tears. Begin to breathe life back into the shattered pieces of my soul. Put me back together again, the way you know my heart and life needs to be.

Journal Your Thoughts Below

_____

_____

_____

_____

_____

_____

_____

_____

_____

_____

_____

_____

_____

_____

_____

_____

_____

_____

Day Three

I waited patiently for the Lord; he turned to me and heard my cry. He lifted me out of the slimy pit, out of the mud and the mire; he set my feet on a rock and gave me a firm place to stand. He put a new song in my mouth, a hymn of praise to our God. Many will see and fear the Lord and put their trust in Him.

PSALM 40:1-3

Will I ever get out of this pit? Will I ever see the light of day? Will I walk around in a fog for the rest of my life? Will it always feel like I am trudging through mud, carefully stepping from one slippery place to the next, wondering if this will be the fall to finally take me out? Will God ever hear my cries and help me?

These were the questions I asked myself on a daily basis when I was trampled by Anxiety Elephants. Every time I pulled myself up from one takedown, I was blindsided by another. It was exhausting, and frankly, there were days the mud and the mire suffocated me. I couldn't breathe. I couldn't function. I couldn't live.

I remember asking God, more often than I would like to admit, if He was really there. I cried out, "Where is the help You promised me all throughout Your Word?" I even got mad at Him and let Him know how angry I felt inside. In today's scripture, it tells us He will lift us up, but there was a time when I felt like I was slowly sinking farther and farther away.

The amazing thing about God is He can handle any concern we throw at Him. He allowed me to go through my emotions and ask Him questions, but He never stopped loving me. He never stopped reaching for me. He never gave up on me.

He hasn't stopped loving you, either. He hasn't stopped reaching for you. He hasn't given up on you.

I know how strong mud and mire feels. I know the scary pit you are in right now. I know the desperate cries coming from your heart and soul. I know the whisper of anxiety telling you, you will never make it out.

But I also know this: if you are *patient*, He will pull you out. He will give you a firm place to stand. He will give you a new song to sing. He will put you in a place where you can help others.

So, how do you remain patient? How can you stay calm when you feel as though you are in a muddy pit being sucked down like quicksand?

We actually need to treat anxiety-ridden feelings the same way we would treat real quicksand or a mud bog. Researchers tell us, if you get pulled down, do the following: relax, take deep breaths, slowly move toward solid ground—inch by inch, and rest. Then REPEAT.

As you cry out to God, you can apply today's steps in patience, while He reaches down to you. By following this process, you will begin to feel God lifting you up and your soul singing a new song! You will feel the amazing pull from the rope of HOPE.

Action Step

How do we keep pushing back Anxiety Elephants when they continually try to knock us down into the mire and the muck? We do it one small step at a time, taking daily action to begin our climb back up. Pick two of the items listed in today's devotional to start working on. Write them down below. Do you need to focus on relaxing and taking deeper breaths? Maybe you need to work on taking smaller steps and giving yourself time to figure out each one. Which two areas will you concentrate on to help you feel the pull out of anxiety quicksand?

Prayer

Dear God, help me to take small daily steps. Thank you for reminding me that these small movements will add up to bigger progress. Show me what I need to focus on today, so I can continue to pull on your rope of Hope. Amen

Journal Your Thoughts Below

_____

_____

_____

_____

_____

_____

_____

_____

_____

_____

_____

_____

_____

_____

_____

_____

_____

_____

Day Four

For God has not given us a spirit of fear; but
one of power, love and a sound mind.

2 TIMOTHY 1:7

Fear.

I can see traces of this enemy woven through different phases of
my life. Sleeping in the dark was a no-go for me even in college,
so I slept with some sort of light on to make me feel like darkness
was not surrounding me. Riding on roller coasters was never on
my "fun list," until I met my husband. I'm pretty sure I cried on
the first one we road together—I was twenty-one.

Fear has been one of the biggest triggers calling Anxiety Elephants
to come and pick on me.

Triggers signal Anxiety Elephants to show up and wreak havoc in
your body, mind, and soul. Unless you are aware of what these
signals are for you, you do not even realize they have been activat-
ed, until the Elephants are already beating you up.

Fear controlled me. I lived in it and it stole my life away. I couldn't leave my house, sleep at night, and I couldn't eat food I loved. Bye, bye doughnuts and pizza.

In 2011, my husband wanted to go to the beach with our then, two-year-old daughter. It was going to be her first trip and my soul was in agony. How could we leave our house? What if she got pulled in by the waves and we couldn't save her? How could we travel deserted roads at night when no one would know where we were? I have to wear a swim suit in front of people?

Irrational fears filled my mind. Tears of terror stained my face. My family's happiness surrounded me, after all, it was my daughter's first time in the sand and water—but my mind was clouded with doubt, worry, and the stings of personal collapse. I could not share their joy in those moments.

Over time, I have learned to recognize when my fear trigger is sending an alarm to the Anxiety Elephants. When that happens, I have to remind myself what type of mind and spirit God has given me. Our Heavenly Father wants us to stand strong against Anxiety Elephants, and in today's passage, Timothy reminds us we do not have a cowardice spirit looming inside. Because of the Fruit of the Spirit (Galatians 5:22-23), which includes love, we can overpower fear. As we walk in God's presence, we walk in the courage of the Lion and the Lamb (Revelations 5:5-6).

What could trigger you? Here are some examples of common issues that signal Anxiety Elephant attacks:

- Stress level increases
- Lack of sleep
- Socializing or lack of socializing (isolation)
- What is going into the body and mind (food, drink, outside influences/messaging)
- Juggling too much at one time

By recognizing your triggers now, you can head off Anxiety Elephants when they come for you.

Action Step

Write down what your triggers are. What sounds the alarm for your Anxiety Elephants? To stomp them out, you need to know what is opening the door to them. Ask God to help you become aware of your triggers and to remember He has given you a sound mind and a spirit filled with power and love. Say to yourself often, "No more FEAR!"

Prayer

Thank you God, for reminding me today that I do not have a spirit of fear, and these triggers in my life do not control me. Help me to walk in what you have given me: power, love, and a sound mind. Amen.

Journal Your Thoughts Below

_____

_____

_____

_____

_____

_____

_____

_____

_____

_____

_____

_____

_____

_____

_____

_____

_____

_____

Day Five

Fear not, for I am with you; be not dismayed, for I am your God; I will strengthen you, I will help you, I will uphold you with my righteous right hand.

ISAIAH 41:10

Fear is a tactic Anxiety Elephants never grow tired of using. It will play tricks on your mind. I like to use the following acronym to describe FEAR: False Evidence Appearing Real. It takes what you see and manipulates it into something completely untrue.

Going to the grocery store made me feel jittery and uneasy. I checked under my car and behind my seat to make sure no one was there waiting for me, like they do on crime shows. This behavior became a new way of life. Driving at night only happened with all my lights on inside the car—I wanted to make sure no dangerous person was in there. I thought, with the lights on, if someone was inside my vehicle, then the other cars driving by would see them and call the police. Crazy I know, but this is where Anxiety Elephants had taken my mind.

How about you? Where have Anxiety Elephants taken your mind in fear?

Fear is used by our enemy, so God equipped us with plenty of scriptures to fight back and stand our ground. God is using today's scripture to remind us exactly WHO He is, and that He is right there with us in the battle.

He let the Israelites know they were not alone. He was with them and He delivered them from their enemies. God gave them exactly what they needed to get through the trials and tribulations they were experiencing. God's people could trust Him.

The same is true for us, His living children. God knows what we are going through and what we need. He wants us to lean on Him and allow Him to hold us up with His righteous right hand, but we have to believe He is there. We have to trust our Heavenly Father is going to do what He said He would do.

Fear tries to tell you something different. It tries to tell you God's Word and promises are not for you. It tells you if you share your trial with someone, they will turn their back on you. Fear tries to convince you that you can't be used by God because you are a broken mess.

Fear is lying to you.

You can be used by God beyond what you could ever think or imagine! Your friends will love you through this trial. You aren't the only one who battles worry. There is HOPE for you. With Christ's help, you CAN outwit Anxiety Elephants.

How do you stand your ground when fear comes silently to your door with a sneak attack?

Begin to speak God's Word out loud and remind fear who your God is. Our scripture today is a great weapon to start with. Write it down and put it where you can see it daily. Memorize it and hide it in your heart. This process may feel awkward to you at first but practicing this strategy will help you feel God's power rise up in you as you declare promises.

When fear says you can't do something, wipe it out by doing the very thing it says you cannot do. It could be going to the store alone or eating by yourself at a restaurant. It could be stepping out in faith in a big way to go after a God-given dream. It could be something as simple as going to bed after you check all your doors one time, verses going back for multiple twists of the handle. By the way, I'm guilty of this, too. Still a work in progress, but I am working on these steps alongside of you.

Finally, cultivate friendships with people you can reach out to and share your fearful thoughts with. I am talking about the type of friends who will tell you they love you, speak life over you, and remind you WHOSE you are. They will encourage you not to let fear push you around any longer. You need friends who will love you enough to tell you the truth and help you get out of those panicky thoughts instead of remaining imprisoned by them.

FEAR NOT.

Action Step

Write today's scripture down and put it somewhere so you can see it constantly. Pick something small you have been afraid to do and go tackle it.

Prayer

Thank you God, that I have nothing to fear with you on my side. Thank you for strengthening me to crush these Anxiety Elephants today. They no longer have power over me. Amen.

Journal Your Thoughts Below

_____

_____

_____

_____

_____

_____

_____

_____

_____

_____

_____

_____

_____

_____

_____

_____

_____

_____

Day Six

Cast all your anxiety on Him because He cares for you.

1 PETER 5:7

Here I am, walking in the middle of the grocery store. I have my baseball cap pulled down as far as it will go, I might have brushed my teeth, and I have zero makeup on my face. I am just praying no one sees me broken. I can hear myself audibly begging God to get me out of a place where there is no good hiding spot. Then here they come—the Anxiety Elephants. I feel a sudden pounding on my chest, coming out of nowhere. My skin turns a flush pink color. Sweat beads are collecting under my hat. Breathing feels impossible as my oxygen intake lessens. I become paralyzed with fear. Questions pour into my mind . . .

WHY are they coming now?

Is there something wrong with me?

Will this ever end?

What will people think of me if they find out?

Maybe you have experienced something like the moment I just described. If you have, I totally get it. When this happens, please know you are not crazy, and you are not the only person this happens to.

One tool that has helped me when Anxiety Elephants show up uninvited, is to cast. When you cast something away from you, it's like you are throwing it as far away as you can. When fishermen went out in the ocean looking for fish during biblical times, they took their nets and threw them out with all their might. This was not a one and done process. Multiple times, they had to cast their nets to reach the fish.

To start casting, I made sure I had paper or a journal with me. When that pounding started, I STOPPED whatever it was I was doing and began writing as fast as I could. Worrying about correct grammar and punctuation marks was not a priority. Sometimes my lines were crooked and words would graze off the page. Appearance did not matter. The goal was simply to get my thoughts and feelings on the page. After I finished writing, I took the paper, wrinkled it up, and even ripped it into pieces, then I cast or threw it away.

Today's verse tells us God cares about you. That means whatever is causing you anxiety or an anxious feeling, matters to Christ. Big or small—CAST it on Him. Throw it at His feet and tell Him what is going on in you. Nothing you say will catch Him off guard. He already knows and it's okay.

Action Step

What do you need to CAST to God today? Take a couple of minutes to tell Him what is causing you to feel anxious. Write it on a piece of paper, then wrinkle it up, and cast/throw it away.

Prayer

Thank you Father, that you love me unconditionally. Help me not to let Anxiety Elephants get the best of me. Holy Spirit, remind me throughout the day to STOP, CAST, and PRAY, and to remember that you are with me. Amen.

Journal Your Thoughts Below

_____

_____

_____

_____

_____

_____

_____

_____

_____

_____

_____

_____

_____

_____

_____

_____

_____

_____

Day Seven

That is why, for Christ's sake, I delight in weaknesses, in insults, in hardships, in persecutions, in difficulties. For when I am weak, then I am strong.

2 CORINTHIANS 12:10

Weakness. I always thought this was a terrible thing. Growing up, I had trained myself not to need any help. Maybe I should say I had trained myself to *think* I did not need any help.

As a young child, I can still remember a boy from my class making fun of me because I had cerebral palsy in my left side. I had a limp and my foot was turned inward. I held my arm up by my side, but I couldn't feel it. The day he gathered our first-grade class around me, hopping like a bunny rabbit, making fun of the way I looked, is a day etched in my brain forever.

My mind told me he was making fun of me because I was weaker than him, and it was a horrible feeling. I drew a line in the sand from that point, determined not to be weak, not to feel that way, and not to need anyone again. I fended for myself.

Throughout my life, I became my own bully when I saw a weakness arise. I didn't need anyone else to push me around. I shamed and belittled myself, because Anxiety Elephants convinced me I had to be perfect. I thought I couldn't make any mistakes, and if I did, no one would accept me. This is a ton of pressure, right? Are you putting pressure on yourself thinking if you make a mistake it is all over for you?

Fast forward thirty years later, and I realized my six-year-old thinking was a bit wrong. I had forgotten about God's grace and its sufficiency in my weakness. His grace is more than enough to cover our frailty. His grace, His unmerited favor to us, is present always. As His children, we cannot lose this beautiful gift.

WE are all weak. WE all have struggles. WE all have our issues. WE are all flawed creatures.

Just as Paul did in today's verse, we need to remember where our help comes from. We do not have to hide our shortcomings and pretend to have it all together. We can boast in them because the beauty of our weakness is where Christ's power and grace become magnified in us and through us.

How do we do this? How do we boast and delight in our weaknesses? How do we make this shift in our thinking?

First, give yourself the same grace God has given you. If you mess up or make a mistake, don't beat yourself up. Stop thinking your entire day is a bust because of one small slip up. Be still in the moment and say to yourself, "Grace."

Second, pray. In those moments when you know you typically shame yourself, pray and talk to God. Ask Him to do exactly what our scripture says, and to be strong where you are weak. Ask Him to let His power overcome those pesky Anxiety Elephants.

Third, reach out to others and ask for help. I know this can be hard, but it is rewarding when you do. If Anxiety Elephants can keep you isolated and quiet, they can keep you in slavery. Once you give yourself grace, start praying and talking to others—it weakens anxiety's grip on you. Freedom is yours when you become open and vulnerable. Who is one person whom you can reach out to and say, "Hey, today is hard for me. Will you pray me through? Will you let me just vent and get all of this out? Will you help me find a scripture to hold on to until this attack is over?"

Friend, you are covered by God's grace. He has removed the shame of anxiety from you. He has accepted you as you are and wants to help you become all He has purposed you to be. It doesn't matter how many times you have fallen—His grace will continue picking you back up.

Wonderful. Amazing. Beautiful. Perfect. Powerful. Life Changing Grace!

Action Step

Begin making shifts in your thinking. Allow grace to permeate your soul. You might simply whisper "Grace" over yourself, or you might pray and talk to the Lord more when anxious moments arise. You may want to find a person who can help you and ask them to walk this road with you. Turn to one or more of today's strategies and allow God to lead you in His Strength.

Prayer

Heavenly Father, thank you for giving me what I do not deserve. Thank you for this gift You have showered upon me. Remind me to give myself this same grace today. You never asked for perfection from me. Help me to stop demanding it from myself. Amen.

Journal Your Thoughts Below

_____

_____

_____

_____

_____

_____

_____

_____

_____

_____

_____

_____

_____

_____

_____

_____

_____

_____

_____

_____

Day Eight

Do not be anxious about anything, but in every situation, by prayer and petition, with thanksgiving, present your requests to God. The peace of God, which transcends all understanding, will guard your hearts and minds in Christ Jesus.

PHILIPPIANS 4:6-7

Getting the kids to school five minutes late because you overslept from not getting enough sleep for three straight days. Getting to work and finishing the project that was due the day before. Cleaning your house so the lady who cleans the house can actually clean the house. Getting home and trying to cook one meal with some sort of vegetable so momfail does not kick in and heap hot coals on your head. It's not even bedtime yet in this scenario, and I'm already overwhelmed by one thing—STRESS! Can anyone relate?

The Anxiety Elephant of stress is one I am still in the process of defeating on a regular basis. This may never go away entirely, but if we learn how to deal with the pressures of life differently, we can keep it at bay.

How do we keep stress levels from triggering our Anxiety Elephants? Today's scripture gives us two weapons to use in our lives: prayer and giving thanks.

Moving from a big city to a somewhat small city was terrifying as a young married couple. Change is overwhelming for me—hello, anxiety! When my husband said he wanted us to pray about moving back to his hometown, so he could start a business, I was scared and confused. I had my dream job and now I had to let it go?

We prayed. Even though I was filled with fear, through prayer God gave me peace about the move. I discovered He had other opportunities I would have missed out on had we not prayed and sought His direction in making this major change on our life map. Thanksgiving replaced my anxious thoughts.

One day, a craving for Strawberry Poppyseed Salad overcame me, so I was on my way to get this deliciousness in my belly. On my short drive over, I was talking with the Lord about how I could give back to a friend who had blessed me with her time and talents. I looked up in my rearview mirror, and she sat behind me in the drive-thru lane. God's answer came quickly to such a pocket-sized request. Once again, thanks filled my heart.

Note, today's scripture does not say the situation we pray and give thanks about has to be big and important. It simply says *every* situation. When our stress levels increase over something that seems minuscule to others, we can pray. When life changing circumstances come up, we can pray. God truly cares about everything we face.

Giving thanks is something I take for granted at times. I get caught up in what I don't have or what's not happening, so I forget how truly blessed I am. Saying bedtime prayers with my youngest keeps me grounded in the art of gratitude. She can spend thirty minutes listing off everything, and I mean everything, she is thankful for in her precious little life. Her list will go from grandparents to having her own potty. How different would life look if we thanked God for every single good thing in our lives—if we remembered to stop and express our appreciation when He answers our prayers? When we tell God what we are grateful for, it is amazing how fast those Anxiety Elephants run the other way.

Action Step

Practice praying about everything in your life. The big and small things. Talk to God like He is sitting right there with you having coffee. Then, thank Him for every good thing in your life. By doing these two things, you will be amazed at how different you feel and how fast you stomp out another Anxiety Elephant.

Prayer

Thank you God, that I can come to you about every situation in my life, no matter the size. Help me, Holy Spirit, to simply pray about everything and have an attitude of gratitude. Amen.

Journal Your Thoughts Below

_____

_____

_____

_____

_____

_____

_____

_____

_____

_____

_____

_____

_____

_____

_____

_____

_____

_____

Day Nine

For we are God's handiwork, created in Christ
Jesus to do good works, which God prepared
beforehand, that we should walk in them.

EPHESIANS 2:10

The human body is an amazing thing, and it's intricately connected to the mind. Both affect how the other functions. Scripture tells us God wove each one of us together in a different but wonderful way.

When I was putting negative thoughts into my mind, it impacted my body. When I told myself I was a failure and not good enough, my head hung lower than Eeyore, and my body felt like the biggest sack of flour you'd find at the store. I had forgotten that God spent time on me, and I was His workmanship—His masterpiece.

What about you? Have you forgotten how much time God spent making you and breathing life into you? When you wake up in the morning, what are the first thoughts and mantras you say to yourself? Are you telling yourself what you are not and who you will never be?

Think about this—the skillful work of our Master Craftsman created every fiber of our beings. We matter so much to him that He made sure we were not a copycat of any other person. YOU are an incredible masterpiece to Him. Not only did He think about every part of you as He was knitting you together, but He was also thinking about His plan in advance for you. He thought about YOUR PURPOSE as He was creating you ON PURPOSE.

God sees the beauty inside of you and moves past the mess with no judgement. He wants you to wipe away the distortion you've built up in your vision of yourself, created from anxiety. Turning a pervasive sense of failure off is going to be a daily task. As difficult as this may be, you are worth the work because you matter, and the works God has prepared for you are important.

To dismantle the failure trigger, you will have to start speaking life over yourself. Your body and mind are listening to you. They interpret your words through actions and reactions. Negative talk breeds negative action. To see a change in your day to day self, change your internal dialogue. Be conscious and intentional with the words you speak to yourself.

You may think, *What if I don't believe these things about myself even though God does?*

This is an honest thought and one I have also been plagued with. I think we can take a lesson from the man who brought his son possessed by an evil spirit to Jesus. In Mark 9:24, we see him telling Jesus to help him overcome his unbelief. For a while, you may find this is part of your daily prayer with Jesus. Going from a defeatist mindset to an overcomer mindset is going to take practice. You will not get this right the first time, nor will you believe initially. Repetition will be your friend, and there's no time like the present to start.

Action Step

Go look in your mirror. Find the scriptures I referenced and read them out loud. Name characteristics you like about yourself. It could be your hair, the way you make people laugh, anything. Tell yourself that you were created for a purpose and a plan (Jeremiah 29:11). Take the negative thoughts captive when they come (2 Corinthians 10:5) and replace them with positive alternatives. Continue to practice writing down scriptures and place them where you will see them to remind yourself what God says about you.

Prayer

God, I am so amazed and thankful that You took your time creating me on purpose for a purpose. Help me to speak words of life over myself today and to believe them. Amen.

Journal Your Thoughts Below

_____

_____

_____

_____

_____

_____

_____

_____

_____

_____

_____

_____

_____

_____

_____

_____

_____

_____

Day Ten

For God did not send His Son into the world to condemn the world, but that the world through Him might be saved.

JOHN 3:17

We all have one bully in our life who never leaves us alone. This bully constantly puts us down. It tells us what we aren't and how we will never measure up to others around us. The words this bully speaks are filled with hatred, and we can barely lift our heads when it comes. It tells us all the things we should be doing, because others are doing them, or that others expect us to be doing them.

This bully can be louder than any cheerleader you have in your life. Are you ready to hear who this bully is, attacking each of us?

It's **you**. Your biggest bully is yourself. We are our own worst critics. All the negative thoughts going on in our minds exhaust us. Statements like:

You will never be as good a mom as she is.

You should be able to get your laundry done, spend time with your kids, have your makeup on point, AND have a home cooked meal ready like all your friends on social media.

You are a burden to so many when you ask for help. You should be able to do it all by yourself.

If people knew you battled anxiety, they would turn their backs on you in a hot minute.

You are a failure.

Shall I keep going, or do any of these bullying statements we say to ourselves ring true for you?

We have to stop "*should-ing*" on ourselves!

Freedom from shame, condemnation, and bullying comes as we read today's scripture. It was never in God's plan to send Jesus here to condemn us all to Hell and tell us how bad and awful we are. His mission was and is the complete opposite. Jesus was sent here to save us. He wants to rescue us. "Us" includes you and me.

How do you stop being your own biggest bully?

Allow the love and forgiveness we find in Jesus to penetrate your heart, mind, and soul. Open the door to Him. Confess Him as your Savior and your Lord and allow Him to be the protector in your life.

Change any malicious thoughts about yourself invading your

mind. Old thought habits are difficult to break, but not impossible. We have to combat those lies with the truth, and God's Word is full of the truth of who we truly are.

Open the Bible and do some research on what it says about you. Look up scriptures you can write down on notecards or in the note section of your phone. Have them with you wherever you go so when the Bully Anxiety Elephant comes, you can pull the truth out to knock it down. The following are great go-to scriptures:

- *I am a friend of Jesus.* (John 15:15)
- *I am justified and redeemed.* (Romans 3:24)
- *I am no longer a slave to sin.* (Romans 6:6)
- *I have been accepted by Christ.* (Romans 15:7)
- *I am chosen, holy, and blameless before God.* (Ephesians 1:4)
- *I was created with a purpose, plan, and hope.* (Jeremiah 29:11)
- *I am God's workmanship created to produce good works.* (Ephesians 2:10)

Finally, let yourself believe. Believe these things are not just true about others, but they are also true for you. God's Word has never changed, and He has never changed His mind about you. He has no plans to humiliate you. Out of love He sent His one and only Son for you. He believes in you. It's time to silence your bully.

Action Step

Use some of the verses referenced above or find some scriptures of your own to help you declare the truth of who you are. Every time the bully comes at you in your mind, fight with TRUTH. This bully needs to be reminded of exactly who you are. Don't back down. Dig your heels in and fight!

Prayer

Thank you Jesus, that you call me Your friend. You have reminded me today I am chosen, holy, and blameless before God. You have given me TRUTH. Help me to not listen to the lies anymore. Amen.

Journal Your Thoughts Below

_____

_____

_____

_____

_____

_____

_____

_____

_____

_____

_____

_____

_____

_____

_____

_____

_____

_____

Day Eleven

For He has not despised the affliction of the
afflicted, and he has not hidden his face from
him, but has heard when he cried to him.

PSALM 22:24

In my deepest battles with anxiety, I wondered if God was there
with me and if He could hear my cries. I often thought if I
despised myself and saw myself as unworthy, He definitely saw
me in the same light. I felt exhausted and alone. I couldn't find
the strength to get up and out from under the Anxiety Elephants
anymore.

My lament to the Lord became faint. The anxiety crippled me,
because my mind and thoughts stayed in the same place 24/7—
tension was all I thought about. It felt like I was behind a prison
wall and I couldn't find my way out.

Have you found yourself in this place with anxiety? Have you
wondered if God hears your plea anymore? Have you thought of
yourself as unworthy of help—especially His?

At this point in the journey, you may need to make a turn or an about-face from the direction you are going. Just as today's scripture tells us, our Abba Father does not despise us or our afflictions. He does not see you as unworthy nor is He ignoring your appeal for help. He isn't playing a hide-and-seek game with you. If you are ready to make a mental shift and hear from Him, it is time to begin the cleaning-out process.

This is such a powerful part of your Anxiety Elephants' stomping quest. They have caused you to press down your troubles for far too long. By holding on to so much, there is no space available for you to hear or feel God. Let go of the distress and affliction anxiety is causing you. Maybe you didn't realize you were gripping it until now, but it's time to release. Once you let those painful emotions go, you will be able to hear the still small voice coming from the Lord.

How does the cleaning-out process work? What do you need to do to get the mud and muck out of you? How do you let go of the affliction? How do you experience freedom?

Seeking professional counseling can be very helpful. Speaking with my doctor and finding a Christian counselor were vital in my healing and helped me overcome the Anxiety Elephants in my life. They showed me how to dig up the causes of my struggle. In getting this kind of support, I was able to release the troubles I'd held in for so long. Without their help, I never would have known the root of my battle with Anxiety Elephants. I would have stayed stuck in the same destructive pattern. Just as seeking professional help for physical problems in our lives benefits us, doing so for our mental health is just as important.

Next, you have to take off the mask—no more hiding and using the beloved slang of "I'm fine." You are not fine. Masks are a burden we were never meant to bear. God loves and accepts you without a mask. Who He has created you to be on the inside is waiting for the real you to come forward. Pull back the layers and allow the beauty within you to shine on your outside.

Going to church and being among a body of believers also helps in the cleaning-out process. When you are in fellowship with God's people, you can feel the Holy Spirit. It will strengthen you and help you hear God's Word as you worship Him alongside others. Sitting in the back on the end of a pew for a quick exit (I did!) is okay. Taking a step of faith by going to church will make a huge difference in cleaning out the muck and mud in your life.

Finally, prayer and worship are cleansing. Prayer is your way to talk to God as a friend because He IS your friend. He is a God who cares about you. Worship is one of the most powerful weapons we have. Find some songs of praise to help you fight your battle against anxiety. It's in worship you realize God is lovingly placing you under the protection of His wings.

Action Step

Unmask yourself—no more hiding. Call your doctor or search for a professional counselor in your area. They will know how to help you. Use your prayer time to cry out to God as you work on this cleaning-out process.

Prayer

Thank You God, for allowing me to come to You without a mask. I am laying these unhealthy habits at Your feet. Lead me to those knowledgeable in my struggle with anxiety. Amen.

Journal Your Thoughts Below

_____

_____

_____

_____

_____

_____

_____

_____

_____

_____

_____

_____

_____

_____

_____

_____

_____

_____

_____

Day Twelve

We demolish arguments and every pretension that sets itself up against the knowledge of God, and we take captive every thought to make it obedient to Christ.

2 CORINTHIANS 10:5

When attacking, Anxiety Elephants can take your thoughts to some absurd places. These ideas are irrational, and yet appear so real in your mind. Once they get planted in your head, they take over and an entire sequence of unfortunate events take place. Before you know it, you are in complete panic mode, unable to breath, unable to move, unable to speak. All this stems from one single thought.

Our minds are powerful. What we think about can affect every part of our lives and the lives of those around us. This is how anxiety can grow into such a stronghold. It's not something anyone can see, so it is easier to conceal. The more we hide our thoughts, the bigger they become. The bigger those thoughts become, the stronger the Anxiety Elephants. As soon as they can, they knock us down. Who knew one single thought could be so powerful? Well, our enemy knew.

What are you thinking about? What are you putting into your brain?

This was a big one for me. My thoughts were all over the place, full of negative things about myself. I constantly put myself down. Nothing I did was ever good enough. I thought about disturbing programs I watched on TV earlier in the day. Watching shows involving crimes and murder were the worst, especially if they involved families or children. I thought about what I would do if those things happened to us, allowing my thoughts to go to the extreme. It was horrifying trying to stop them.

I had to intentionally change what I was thinking about to remove the anxious thoughts that were sucking the life right out of me. This was a step which took consistency. I had to try over and over again until I got into the habit of thinking differently.

As you begin to change your thoughts remember: give yourself time and grace. Overcoming anxiety is not an overnight fix. In the beginning, you will mess up more often than not. Once you get the hang of taking those thoughts captive, it will happen so quickly the Anxiety Elephants won't know what hit them.

How do you start? How do you change your thoughts?

STOP. Stop by your actions or say *stop* in your head. Don't let the thoughts coming into your mind take root. Accept ownership to stop them. When you keep negative thoughts from settling in, you keep them from growing in you.

After you **STOP** anxious thoughts from taking root, you have to take them **CAPTIVE.** It would be great if they played nice and stopped when we told them, but it won't be that easy. Anxiety will still try to creep back in if we don't take it *CAPTIVE.* The best way to capture anxious thoughts, is to write all of your feelings down. Document what's bombarding your mind. Write until you can no longer hear your fears.

Finally, **REPLACE** old thoughts with new ones. The effort you put forth in stopping your old thoughts, taking them captive, and throwing them away is a great start. But replacing those thoughts is key. If we don't put something else in our minds, we are left with empty space. Eventually, this space fills up once again with anxious thoughts, but this time, they will double or triple in number. Put new thoughts in your brain by writing down positive statements about yourself. Include life-giving scripture from God's Word. Say these things out loud so your mind hears the shift you have made in your heart.

The practice outlined above will help you grow stronger against Anxiety Elephants. They will no longer be able to use your mind against you. You can now call on your thoughts to fight back against them.

Action Step

What are you thinking about? Keep paper with you. When you feel those bad thoughts come in, practice stopping, taking those thoughts captive, and replacing them. You can write down the old thoughts and scratch them out or throw them away. Document a new, positive thought and read it out loud. Read it, believe it, and receive it!

Prayer

Lord, help me to take bad thoughts captive today. Quicken my spirit when those negative thoughts come, so I can replace them with life-giving truth instead! Amen.

Journal Your Thoughts Below

_____

_____

_____

_____

_____

_____

_____

_____

_____

_____

_____

_____

_____

_____

_____

_____

_____

_____

Day Thirteen

For you created my inmost being; you knit me together in my mother's womb. I praise you because I am fearfully and wonderfully made; your works are wonderful, I know that full well.

PSALM 139:13-14

When you are in the middle of an anxiety attack, the last thing that you feel is fearfully and wonderfully made, right? Most of the time you feel quite the opposite. The whispers of Anxiety Elephants sound like screams between your ears. They certainly aren't calling you pleasant names to make you smile from ear to ear. Instead, they use phrases like the following to bring a numbing expression on your face:

- *You are a waste of time.*
- *You are a failure.*
- *You are a disappointment.*
- *You are a burden to everyone around you.*
- *You do not have a purpose because you can't get past this.*
- *You are just taking up space.*

- *You are less than.*
- *You will never come out of this pit.*
- *You do not matter.*
- *You were a mistake.*

Whatever the trigger word or statement is for you, Anxiety Elephants will put it on repeat in your head. Hidden, so no one else can see, they attack invisibly. Anxiety Elephants go after our minds because they know the power of a single thought. They know we go where our minds take us. If they can plant thoughts of doubt, fear, and shame, then worth-reducing phrases become more believable to us.

Personally, my trigger word was FAILURE. I was paralyzed by this word, this thought. Am I failing my family? Am I a failure to my church? Have I failed God? Every day those thoughts punched me in the gut and emotionally knocked me down. I was afraid to move or do anything at all because I didn't want to fail. Anxiety paralyzes you so you can't live your life in freedom. Anxiety Elephants know the power of faith, so they remain relentless in their attacks attempting to weaken your trust in God.

It is tiresome to get up and live like this every day. It is not what God wants or desires for us. How do I know this from today's scripture? God would not have spent time knitting us together in our mother's wombs if He didn't have a specific purpose for each one of us (Psalm 139). He established purpose in us while He took His time creating us. He breathed His breath into our lungs. Wow! The breath of God is inside us. The power of God is inside us. The purpose and plans of God are inside us.

When your trigger words and statements come, take a deep breath in and out as often as you need to, until you remember it is God's breath in your lungs. Dwell on the truth that your Heavenly Father sees *you* as fearfully and wonderfully made. Ask Him to help you see the purpose and work He created for you. Speak life over yourself. If all you can do is replace negative thoughts with scripture, then this is a step in the right direction to counteract the attack of Anxiety Elephants. You are one step closer to walking in victory!

Action Step

Practice doing all of today's steps together. Sometimes, just taking deep breaths are enough to push back those trigger words. Other times, the attacks are more severe, and you have to go through all of the steps. The main thing is perseverance. Refuse to quit. No longer live in the lie that you aren't enough. Choose to believe you are fearfully and wonderfully made.

Prayer

Thank you God, for the reminder that I am fearfully and wonderfully made. Help me to believe this and receive it. Amen.

Journal Your Thoughts Below

_____

_____

_____

_____

_____

_____

_____

_____

_____

_____

_____

_____

_____

_____

_____

_____

_____

_____

Day Fourteen

When you lie down, you will not be afraid,
when you lie down, your sleep will be sweet.

PROVERBS 3:24

O sleep, sleep! Wherefore art thou sleep? Why do you leave me searching for you night after night?

Crawling into a warm and cozy bed should be a pleasant experience. A day full of production and accomplishment should be crowned with covers of rest and grace. But for many, going to bed is more of a punishment, so you take your time getting in, knowing the dark places your nightmares are about to carry you. Every night, I would lay down, get still, and then my mind began to race. Fearful thoughts filed in one right after another in perfect synchronization. Pure exhaustion from the day before set in. Worry ate me up inside. There was no off switch. It was a vicious cycle while I ran on this hamster wheel in my head.

I knew I needed rest, but I just could not find it. It's as if Anxiety Elephants took on traits of the Energizer Bunny in my mind.

They kept me going…and going…and going…and going. Trying to silence them in my own strength was not happening. What strength I had left, was beginning to fade as delirium set in.

Not only was my sleep hijacked, but every aspect of my life was hampered from the insomnia. I literally lived on the edge. Maybe you have found yourself there, too. Driving is a task because your vision becomes blurry. Work takes double the time because your mind cannot focus on a small to-do list. Emotions run rampant and are on high alert. You may yell for no apparent reason. Crying may have become a hobby for you. All of this stems from lack of a deep sleep.

So, what did I do to find the sweet slumber my body and mind longed for? First, I made simple changes in what I watched. Criminal Minds could no longer be must-see TV for me. Laughter really is medicine to the soul. I watched classics like *I Love Lucy* and *The Andy Griffith Show*. They don't make em' like they used to. Don't be afraid to grab a blast from the past.

Secondly, I found scriptures on thoughts and rest. Searching for what God's Word had to say about my sleep was another tender reminder of how He cares about every aspect of our lives. I wrote scriptures down, memorized them, and said them out loud. The scripture I shared with you today, was the one I clung to at night, and still do.

Finally, I talked to my doctor. In complete transparency, this was the hardest step for me to take. A battle was waging in my mind. Am I truly trusting God by going to my doctor? Should I just pray harder? Read more Bible stories? Is there really something medically going on keeping me from getting the rest my body is yearning for? God gently reminded me if I was having heart disease or any other physical ailment, I would seek a doctor's expertise. I would not hesitate. God gave me peace and courage to pursue medical advice and use the medicine my physician suggested in the window of time she mapped out. You know what? It helped me! Sleep no longer became a distant memory.

Know God wants you to rest. He doesn't want you to play tug-of-war night after night. He wants your sleep to be sweet. Are you ready to make some changes? Is it time to seek help? How can His Word become the Sword of Truth you need to slay the Anxiety Elephants stealing a pleasant night's rest from you?

Action Step

Maybe you are desperately looking for sleep. You may feel so exhausted you can barely function. Try changing one show you watch on TV. Don't forget—it is okay to ask for help and make these little shifts in your life in order to make big changes happen.

Prayer

Father, I am so tired. I can't do this anymore. I need Your help. I am believing for sweet sleep tonight. Help me cling to your Word and make little changes, so I can see big changes happen. Amen.

Journal Your Thoughts Below

_____

_____

_____

_____

_____

_____

_____

_____

_____

_____

_____

_____

_____

_____

_____

_____

_____

_____

_____

Day Fifteen

But He said to me, "My grace is sufficient for you, for my power is made perfect in weakness." Therefore I will boast all the more gladly about my weaknesses, so that Christ's power may rest on me.

2 Corinthians 12:9

I am not enough.

How could I allow myself to feel and act this way?

Why am I not trusting God?

How can God use somebody like me who deals with something like this?

I am a disappointment to God and to those around me.

Have you ever had ungracious thoughts about yourself? The list above includes things I told myself daily. I woke up persecuting myself and would go to bed doing the same thing. I never knew if it was a sunny or cloudy day, because I never looked up. My eyes were always set on the ground beneath me. There seemed to be a sign above my head blinking my trigger word I have already mentioned, *FAILURE*, for the world to see. Perfection was the only option I gave myself. Grace wasn't for someone like me. At this point, hope was lost from my gaze—or so I thought.

Praise God I was wrong.

Today's message is for all the perfectionists out there. I know what it is like to read devotions every morning and then put myself down because I just can't seem to "get it right." When the goal of perfection is not reached, what happens? Who wants to give up? The enemy is good at making us feel like we will never meet the standard. He made me walk away from opportunities where I really could do something amazing, friendships that held my feet to the fire, and God-given dreams I thought I wasn't good enough to accomplish. I want to stop him from doing the same to you.

God wants you to know He has grace for you, so accept it. He wants you to see yourself the way He sees you. In His eyes, you are not a hot mess who will never get it right. He sees His child who desperately wants to move forward. His desire is that you would stop saying horrible things about His beloved family member.

Maybe today has been a battle for you. If so, just breathe. The fact that you opened this devotional and are ready to stomp out Anxiety Elephants is a win! Instead of looking at where you are not, take a look back and see where you once were. Consider how far you've come.

Rest in His grace today. No more belittling. He loves you where you are. He will love you through this journey and get you where He wants to take you. He has not given up on you, so don't give up on yourself.

Action Step

Write down some of your wins below. Take a moment and realize you are not where you were and celebrate the victory in where you are.

Prayer

Thank you God, for your amazing grace. Help me to receive the acceptance You freely offer, and to celebrate my victories. Amen.

Journal Your Thoughts Below

_____

_____

_____

_____

_____

_____

_____

_____

_____

_____

_____

_____

_____

_____

_____

_____

_____

Day Sixteen

For she said to herself, "If I only touch his garment, I will be made well." Jesus turned, and seeing her he said, "Take heart daughter, your faith has made you well."

MATTHEW 9:21-22

Twelve years—she suffered for twelve years. The woman with an issue of blood going on inside her body that no one understood. No human being could relate to what she was going through. No one could fathom the fear and emotions she had dealt with through her struggle. Doctors could not help her. Family and friends turned their backs on her. Her culture defined her as unclean and unwanted.

Can you identify with any aspect of this woman's story?

Have you dealt with Anxiety Elephants for years and found nothing and no one to help? Have people turned their backs on you and criticized the struggle you face? Have you done just as this woman did and hidden in your shame and guilt? Are you walking around in a mental prison just as she was imprisoned in her own home?

As you read this, you may be thinking or screaming YES to all of these questions. Maybe you have tears streaming down your face because you feel like this woman's story is your story. It cuts right to your heart and right to your issues.

I know this pain runs deep, but I hope you feel the healing balm of hope in today's scripture as well.

In these verses, this woman is all alone and at the end of her rope of hope. She hears this man, Jesus, is coming. She knows about the miracles He has done. Stepping out of her confinement, she is choosing to believe He can set her free.

She risked it all, down to her life, for this moment. Because she was considered unclean at that time, anything and everyone she touched was also considered unclean. This is why it was such a huge risk for her to be out in this crowd. Anyone she may have brushed with her shoulder, had they known who she was and what she dealt with, could have made a scene. In the eyes of the Law, by touching her, Jesus would have also been considered unclean. But in her desperation, all she could think about was her desire to touch the hem of His garment, receive healing, and then going on about her life. She dared to believe.

Shame had such a hold on this woman, that she did not want to address Christ publicly. She wanted to make her move in secret. Anxiety has done the same to us. It has filled us with shame, so we are afraid to admit publicly we need help or a healing touch.

Even in her secrecy, Jesus does not shun her. He does not stop the powerful energy from leaving His body. Reaching out and touching His garment in faith brings instant healing for this hurting human being. He made her whole. He made her new. He restored the broken places in her.

Not only did He do this, but He gave her a new name. Jesus felt the healing power leave His body and asked who touched Him. Now, His disciples thought this was a ridiculous question. They were in a huge crowd. In their eyes, everyone was touching Jesus. They did not realize what had happened.

But at Christ's question, the woman fell to the ground and confessed. She chose not to hide anymore. Jesus didn't expose her out of ill will or malice. He wanted to acknowledge the incredible step of faith she had taken. She was no longer called unclean. Now, she was called DAUGHTER.

Make no mistake, friends. Just as you may relate to the beginning of this woman's story, you can also find a way to identify with the ending. Jesus was very clear when He said her faith made her whole. Small actions of faith, even in her weakness, is what healed the woman. This power is available to us.

Faith is a scary and amazing concept. Reaching out to Jesus in faith can move mountains. Even the mountains looking like elephants.

Today is your day. This is your moment to risk it all and reach out in faith. Ask God to help you overcome Anxiety Elephants. Ask Him to send people across your path who can help you. Ask Him to give you courage to come out of the mental prison you have been in for so long. A tiny mustard seed of faith is more powerful than a big boulder of fear. An act of trust may not seem like much to you, but it is a big beginning. God rejoices in your seedling faith—tiny as it may be.

Action Step

Reach out in FAITH today and ask Jesus to heal you and help you overcome this anxiety. That simple step is huge. You may have to ask multiple times, and you may even have to ask Him to help your unbelief as we have previously talked about. But He will do it. God will acknowledge your faith just as He did with this woman. You are His child and He is ready to heal you.

Prayer

God, I am taking a risk and asking you to do what only You can do in my heart and mind. Give me what I need to escape the crushing feet of Anxiety Elephants. I am reaching out in faith asking you, Father, to bring healing. Amen.

Journal Your Thoughts Below

_____

_____

_____

_____

_____

_____

_____

_____

_____

_____

_____

_____

_____

_____

_____

_____

_____

_____

Day Seventeen

Carry one another's burdens and so fulfill the law of Christ.

GALATIANS 6:2

"Please HELP me." Her text message stopped me in my tracks. She was sitting alone in her apartment at college, and life overwhelmed her. She found herself in the very place we had been talking about over the last couple of weeks—no sleep, rapid heart rate, isolation, and a soul torn in half. Her plea culminated with these words, "I don't understand how I got to this place so I'm reaching out—I need help."

This cry came from someone desperate—desperate for HELP. Walls had come down. A breech had been made in this person's protective barrier, the one they'd held up for so long. This human being didn't want to be alone and could only stand back up with the pull of others lifting her. She'd moved beyond her pride and searched for relief.

Few of us actually ask each other for help, and I am the ring leader of this problem. Maybe like me, you have convinced yourself you are supposed to figure life out on your own. Or maybe you think you should have zero problems and should reflect the picture-perfect social media life everyone else portrays.

LIES…it is all lies, I tell you! No one has a perfect life. We are all so busy wearing our masks of perfection, and it allows Anxiety Elephants to get away with their destructive party.

When I took down my mask and admitted I needed help, it was one of the most freeing feelings. My fear of being looked at differently or shunned—disappeared. No one judged me like I thought they would. They loved me through it. People threw me a lifeline and helped me get up out of the muck and mud I had sunk in. I even discovered I had other friends dealing with the same Anxiety Elephants as me. Peace filled our hearts and minds once we realized we were not alone in our battles.

Your list of helpers may look different than mine, and that is okay. My husband, doctor, counselor, family, and friends were the group I was able to reach out to first. The most important thing is to have those people in your life you can ask for help. I know it is hard, but you are worth it.

Action Step

Share your burdens with those around you and ask for help. This is going to be hard, but you can do this. It could mean asking for prayer, making an appointment with your doctor or counselor, or inviting a friend to come over for coffee so you can talk. Let someone HELP carry your burdens today just as God's Word calls us to do.

Prayer

God, thank you that you did not make us to carry our burdens alone. You want us to let people in to help lighten our load. I confess I am not good at asking for help. Give me the courage today to reach out and ask for support because I am tired of wearing this mask and carrying this weight by myself. Amen.

Journal Your Thoughts Below

_____

_____

_____

_____

_____

_____

_____

_____

_____

_____

_____

_____

_____

_____

_____

Day Eighteen

The Lord your God is in your midst, a mighty
one who will save; he will rejoice over you with
gladness; he will quiet you by his love; he will
exult over you with loud singing.

ZEPHANIAH 3:17

What a beautiful scripture. It's Zephaniah 3:17 God uses to lift
my head up in victory and prevent defeat from keeping me paralyzed. Yes, there are still times Anxiety Elephants knock me down,
and I wonder how in the world I will get back up from the war
they have waged.

Sit and ponder today's verse with me. Go back and read it again
and put your name everywhere you see the word "you." How did
the verse become more personal and real to you?

"The Lord our God is in our midst." Wherever you are, He is
there. He is right there with you. It could be in a pit or a dirty
kitchen floor. Carlines going on for days or the grocery check-out

line. He is there, even when you are sitting in the seat at church wondering if you are going this road alone.

"He is Mighty and He WILL save!" I pray this makes hope resonate inside you. It may look like you will never get past Anxiety Elephants and you won't ever overcome—but those thoughts are lies. Today's scripture shows us something different. Grab hope and put it in your mind and heart; He is MIGHTY. He WILL save you. He is more powerful than those anxious reflections and angst. His timing and way may not look like ours, but ultimately, He will rescue us.

He is rejoicing over you with gladness! He feels great joy and delight in you. It doesn't matter your situation or your circumstance. Your Heavenly Father is captivated by you. He created you in His image. Everything He created, He called good—this includes you.

God is quieting the trembling inside us with His unconditional love. He takes it one step further and exalts over us with loud singing—not a quiet whisper. He is singing passionately and rejoicing over each and every one of us. We are precious in His sight (Isaiah 43:4). The apple of His eye (Psalm 17:8). He holds no sin against us but forgives us and casts it as far as the east is from the west (Psalm 103:12). God's singing over you doesn't stop because anxiety may come in.

Abba Father wants to quiet your anxiety with His love. Press in to this truth—in to His love. He is not going to stop singing and rejoicing over you. He wants you to come and sit in His lap. He wants to hold you just as a parent holds a precious baby and sings sweet songs over them to calm them. This is what your Heavenly Father wants to do for you today.

Action Step

Begin to pray and ask God to reveal His presence in your midst. Ask to sit at His feet. You may weep, or laugh in joy, or breathe the deepest breath you have felt in a long time. He will reveal Himself to each one of us differently. Linger in His presence. Write down what He reveals—what He sings over you—to remind you how He sees you. Nothing can take away your Father's care, not even a stinky elephant.

Prayer

God, I humbly ask You to reveal Yourself to me. Allow me to experience You in these quiet moments. I am waiting to meet with You. Amen.

Journal Your Thoughts Below

_____

_____

_____

_____

_____

_____

_____

_____

_____

_____

_____

_____

_____

_____

_____

_____

Day Nineteen

Be strong and courageous. Do not fear or be in dread of them, for it is the Lord your God who goes with you. He will not leave you or forsake you.

DEUTERONOMY 31:6

Here we go again—the rumbling of elephants is behind you coming in a stampede. Heart pounding, you start running emotionally, but stop in complete dread of what is about to happen. You are not strong or courageous in this moment. Instead, you are overcome with complete fear. I had to rewrite this section at least five times. It is hard for me to admit I lived my life in this way, but I know I have to share my experiences because someone out there can relate.

Isolation and uneasiness consumed me in my battles with Anxiety Elephants. Do you feel despair overtaking you and pushing you into a dark hole where you feel isolated? When you are alone physically and mentally, fear becomes a dangerous thing. It doesn't have to yell at you—all it has to do is whisper, and you are done.

You are not just living in fear, but you are now living in dread. Dread is when you anticipate something is going to happen—real or imagined—with great angst. You may have envisioned every last detail of a fictional scenario that hasn't taken place, but in your mind, it could. Moments like these make you feel completely solitary. You hide yourself because you do not want anyone to know what is going on in your mind. You have taken fear to an extreme level in this mental state.

If I've just described you in any way, I have good news to share. I understand. You are terrified to share this with anyone, so you push your fears and anxious thoughts down. But God knows everything going through your head. He knows the dread sucking the life out of you. He knows and He is still with you. He has not turned His back on you, not once. He hasn't left you. You may have pushed away from Him because you are ashamed of where you are, but your Good Father never left you.

Moses reminds the Israelites of this in today's scripture. God will go with them in all the battles they will face. He does not expect them to face those things alone. This is true for us. He is walking through our battles with us. He wants us to depend on His strength and His promises. He wants us to relinquish control. We were never meant to defeat Anxiety Elephants by ourselves. That's why it doesn't work when we try to work in our own strength.

How do you go from dread to courage?

First, call out the untruth Anxiety Elephants try to feed you. God has not abandoned you. Remind them He has not left you or forsaken you. He has gone before you AND is walking with you.

Finally, don't stop moving. Don't let them paralyze you with fear. Act in faith. Even if it is at a snail's pace, keep moving forward.

Do these steps over and over until you create a new habit. New habits will bring new courage. New courage will bring new faith. New faith will bring new hope. New hope will bring new life.

God is with you. Keep moving!

Action Step

Choose to walk in courage to create new habits. Remind yourself that God is walking with you no matter what untruth Anxiety Elephants may speak. Keep today's verse close to your heart as you move forward, remembering that God will never leave you or forsake you.

Prayer

Thank you God, that I no longer have to live in dread! Fear no longer has a hold on me. Help me to keep moving in courage, even if it feels like I'm progressing in slow motion. Amen.

Journal Your Thoughts Below

_____

_____

_____

_____

_____

_____

_____

_____

_____

_____

_____

_____

_____

_____

_____

_____

_____

_____

Day Twenty

An anxious heart weighs a man down, but a
kind word cheers him up.

PROVERBS 12:25

I sat on the couch in my living room watching TV, when BAM!
Here came the Anxiety Elephants. They threw themselves on me
with such great weight, I could not move. Paralysis overtook my
body. I desperately wanted to move, but I was frozen by the heaviness of it all and the terror of what it might do to me. I felt as if I
would break into a million pieces if I flinched.

Anxiety is so overwhelming, you can't breathe. What breath you
do get out, is very shallow. It can be crippling. It keeps you from
enjoying your life and living it to the fullest. Have you found
yourself in this place?

I already felt broken that day on my couch. Trying to hide my
pain gave anxiety even more power over me. Honestly, I thought
my superpower was to try and keep everything bottled up and

deal with it alone. But my solo struggle was actually more like my kryptonite.

The closer you hold anxiety to your heart, the more power you are giving it over your life. It weakens you, crushing you little by little. It wants to isolate you because it knows if you are not around anyone else, no support or encouragement are spoken over you.

If Anxiety Elephants have pulled you into this place of isolation, it is because they want to take you into an even darker pit of despair. They want to take all hope away from you. I know this because they took me there. Depression can sometimes be a friend of Anxiety Elephants—you may battle both. The two together, depression and anxiety, often feel impossible to defeat.

The first step to getting out from under the heavy weight of depression and anxiety is to lay them down at the feet of Jesus. Verbally confess the pain you are carrying and your efforts to try and fix it alone. My confession included telling Christ I was sorry for my spirit of pride, which was the "why" for me behind my load of anxiety. When you take the step of confessing your "why" you will loosen anxiety's grip on you and receive forgiveness.

The second step after confessing and receiving God's forgiveness, is to forgive yourself. If God can forgive you and cast the weight of guilt far, far away, you can do the same. Remember, perfection was not something He ever expected from you, so take the burden of perfection off of yourself.

Third, start rebuilding your community. Maybe you have pushed people away and closed yourself off. If so, it is time to relearn how to have friends and be a friend. Friendship isn't just listening to their concerns and giving people encouragement. It is also sharing your life and burdens and allowing them to build you up. Being vulnerable with people can be scary. But the beauty in the scariness of vulnerability brings life-changing moments.

Prayer is the final step. Maybe you are praying earnestly day and night for God to help you and pull you out of the pit. Ask yourself this: are you also staying isolated out of pride, afraid to humble yourself and ask others for prayer? You don't have to wait on someone else to ask you if you need prayer for anything. You are not bothering people by requesting prayer. Your community wants to pray for you. Family and friends love you and you matter to them. Prayer changes things, sweet friend, and it's time for things to change.

Action Step

It's time for you to hear this. Allow forgiveness to mend your broken heart. Rebuild your community and let your prayers warriors come into your secret place. Don't rush this step. It is going to be a pivotal changing point in your journey. I am praying for you as you step into this part of the process. I can't wait for you to feel the freedom from allowing others to help carry your heavy weight.

Prayer

Jesus, I ask your forgiveness. I've carried these Anxiety Elephants for this reason: (fill in the blank). I receive your forgiveness. Help me to forgive myself. Show me the people You have prepared to be in my community of support. Amen.

Journal Your Thoughts Below

_____

_____

_____

_____

_____

_____

_____

_____

_____

_____

_____

_____

_____

_____

_____

_____

_____

_____

Day Twenty-One

So God blessed the seventh day and made it
holy, because on it God rested from all his work
that he had done in creation.

Genesis 2:3

I am so excited you have made it to this day! I am giving you
permission to do something you rarely allow yourself to do. Are
you ready for it?

Drum roll please . . .

Today, I officially give you permission to REST!!! I know, you are
probably jumping up and down bursting with excitement. Or,
you are sitting there reading this and saying to yourself, "Really?
She just gave me permission to rest? Is that it? Is that all?!?"

Yes—but wait until you hear everything I want to share.

We have somehow convinced ourselves that rest is a bad thing.
We have put rest and laziness in the same category. But they are

not the same at all. To be lazy is to be unwilling to work, to avoid work, to be reluctant to do anything, or simply to stay idle.

Resting, on the other hand, is giving yourself a moment—some time to relax and recover. Rest is needed for the body to renew its strength. Rest is needed to do the good works God created us to do, as Ephesians 2:10 tells us. Rest allows your brain to get out of overdrive, which is where Anxiety Elephants find an open door to come in and disrupt your mind, body, and soul.

Anxiety Elephants use busyness to overwhelm us and make us think we are being lazy if we aren't active with all things, and I mean ALL the things that come to our minds. They have convinced us we are doing something wrong if we have any free time.

Here's the deal: if the God of all creation took a rest, and made it clear in His Word He rested an entire day, why on earth have we convinced ourselves we can't even take thirty minutes to do the same? If *HE* rested, how much more do you and I need rest?

When God took this rest, He stopped. He was still. In stillness, He was able to look at all He had done and He saw it was good.

When we rest, we can follow His example. We can take a moment and reflect on our day and what we have done. You don't have to talk or write in this time of rest. Be quiet and listen. Give your mind some down-time.

I have found my best rest comes when I disconnect, turning off the phone, computer, and social media. Maybe you need to try this for a day, a week, or a month. You can decide what is best for you.

Try taking a nap. Napping allows your body to do what it can't do while you are awake and moving around. Give yourself time to be restored mentally and physically. Even going to bed thirty minutes to an hour earlier a couple of times a week, can do the same thing.

Finally, make margin in your schedule. Notice, when you read books, or even this devotional, the words do not fill the entirety of the page. There is margin or space, to give your eyes and brain a break. You need a break in your schedule. You need margin in your life. What is something you can take out? What is something you can say no to in order to gain space for rest?

Rest today in God's presence. Take a pause and reflect on Him and His love and kindness. By getting into the practice of resting, you are adding another weapon in your defense against Anxiety Elephants.

Action Step

REST. Pick one of the ways I mentioned above to put rest into practice. It can be disconnecting, taking a nap, taking a walk outside, going to bed earlier, or making margin happen in your schedule. Pick one and watch how a simple task of rest can change so much in your life.

Prayer

Help me to simply disconnect and rest, Lord. Thank You that rest brings restoration. Amen.

Journal Your Thoughts Below

_____

_____

_____

_____

_____

_____

_____

_____

_____

_____

_____

_____

_____

_____

_____

_____

_____

_____

Day Twenty-Two

Because she thought, "If I just touch his clothes, I will be healed." Immediately her bleeding stopped and she felt in her body that she was freed from her suffering.

MARK 5:28-29

The story of the woman with the issue of blood has spoken so much to me over the last few years. Because of this, I want to revisit her story. I have tried to put myself in her place. Her story looks a lot like ours—those of us who have or are battling anxiety.

We don't hear much at all about the people she was around for those twelve years. We do know in verse 26 that she suffered a great deal under the hands of doctors, and they took all her money. Plus, they made her worse! Not a very positive crowd to be hanging around. I can only imagine the negative things they spoke over her to keep her in constant misery.

Twelve years this woman lived in isolation because of this disease. Being in this aloneness may have given her ample time to wallow in negative thoughts. Giving attention to things such as worry, rejection, doubt, and humiliation could have easily been a part of her daily life. She was already seen as dirty, different, useless, and purposeless. She was a prisoner within her home and her mind.

Anxiety works the same way. It is an inward struggle when negative voices and thoughts have influence over our lives. Unfortunately, we get comfortable with the falsehoods spoken from others or ourselves. Anxiety Elephants take those words and use them as ammunition against us.

We can learn something from the woman with the blood issue. She was willing to get uncomfortable.

She hears Jesus of Nazareth is coming to her town. She has heard of His miracles and His love for people. She knows leaving her home means risking her life. She has been comfortable in her misery and stigma, but she knows healing and change will not take place there. For her life to transform, she has to modify her action plan. She has to take the initiative to step out of her comfort zone.

Envision how terrified she was pressing up against everyone in the crowd to get to Jesus and see her determination. She refused to quit. This woman made it to Him and reached out in her faith and touched His robe because she believed by touching the hem of His garment, she would be healed and made whole.

What would have happened to her if she would have remained in a negative space? If comfort was her goal, would she have ever received healing?

Getting uncomfortable is not enjoyable but it is necessary in stomping out Anxiety Elephants. That may not be something you want to read, but I care too much about you not to speak the truth in love. Changing negative thoughts and influences in your life is a critical component.

Evaluate your life. What are you thinking on during the day? What do you do when you have free time? Music that you listen to—is it edifying lyrics or words you might not want others to know you hear? What type of people are you hanging around? Do they speak in a demeaning way towards you?

You may not realize it, but all of these things can give a spark to Anxiety Elephants. They can intensify their attack with the bad seeds being ingrained into your spirit. They use your complacency against you.

Friend, just as this woman stepped out of her comfort zone, God is calling you to do the same. After taking an assessment of your life, you could discover a lot of adjustments that need to be made. You may find yourself choosing different activities. Your taste in music will drastically be different. Reading could even become a new hobby for you. Don't be afraid to put boundaries up with people who degrade you and are unsupportive of the changes you are making.

Are you ready? It's time to get uncomfortable.

Action Step

This lady went after her healing. She had to get uncomfortable to receive it. She knew to transform, she had to make a change. What are the changes you are ready to make in your life? Write them down below. In faith, reach out and ask God to help you take necessary steps. Ask Him to help you trust Him in this uncomfortable place.

Prayer

Dear God, help me to get uncomfortable. Help me do the hard things to make the changes I need to make so I can continue stomping out Anxiety Elephants trying to wreak havoc on me. I am ready. Amen.

Journal Your Thoughts Below

Day Twenty-Three

Trust in the Lord with all your heart, and do not lean on your own understanding. In all your way acknowledge Him, and He will make your paths straight.

PROVERBS 3:5-6

Confession time. I am a major control freak. After saying this to you, I totally breathed a sigh of relief just now. I am pretty sure some of you reading will be in this category with me. Come on—you know you need to make a confession, too.

I try to control everything. I keep my family's schedules and routines the same almost daily. For example, we leave our house at 7:31 a.m. to get my daughters to school on time. If I leave one minute early or one minute late, I panic. If my husband drives a different way to church or another familiar place, I become hysterical, because I have no idea where he is going. Why would he change the route? What is wrong with the way we have always gone? Does he know something I don't know?

This confession is slightly more embarrassing, but I feel like we have been through a lot over the previous pages so why hold back now? Here goes. I will even look up the ending to a movie we are going to watch, so I can control my response. I hate being caught off guard, so by looking ahead, I'll know if it is a happy or sad ending, and I won't be overly emotional. Now, don't worry—I don't share the ending with others and ruin it for them.

At this point, you guys are either laughing at me, laughing with me, or laughing at yourself because you do some of the same things.

Human beings generally feel as if our way and our own understanding are right. If our life doesn't go the way we think it should go or if a kink is thrown into our plans, what do we do? We freak out. We go into catastrophe mode. We panic and freely open the gate to let Anxiety Elephants come in and add fuel to the fire WE started from overthinking and chronic worry.

This was a hard message for me to receive from the Lord. I honestly thought I was innocent. How could little ole me do something wrong? I believed the Anxiety Elephants just wanted to pick on me.

Yes, they do want to pick on us, but we have to remember we are not perfect. Some of the anxiety we experience, at times, is there because we have put ourselves in those situations. Confession is a beautiful medicine for the soul.

Once I confessed my need to "pilot the plane" if you will, and asked God to forgive me for thinking I knew a better route for my life than He did, I felt peace. I felt His forgiveness. I began to really understand I didn't have control of everything and actually, He intended life to be this way.

You can take pressure off of yourself today. Not everything that happens is supposed to be under your control and in a way you understand. God has a better view for your life. You can trust in what He sees. Acknowledge Him and seek Him first. You do not have to figure it out on your own anymore.

Talk to your Father and follow His advice. Ask Him how He wants you to fight back when Anxiety Elephants come at you. Acknowledge He is God, you are not, and tell Him you are trusting Him to be your guide. It's time to give Him back the controls.

Action Step

Confession. It really is good for your soul. We all have sinned and fallen short of the glory of God (Romans 3:23). You are not the only one. You may have done this at the beginning of these thirty-one days, but it could be that God has revealed other areas where you need His forgiveness. Maybe you realize you need forgiveness for being prideful, being untrusting of Him, or trying to decide on your own which way your life should go instead of asking Him first. Feel free to use the space below to write out your confession.

Prayer

Thank you for the reminder once again, Lord, about the power of confession. There is nothing I can hide from You. You know it all and still love me. Thank you for forgiveness. Continue to guide my steps Lord. You are the Pilot of this life—help me to enjoy the ride. Amen.

Journal Your Thoughts Below

Day Twenty-Four

When anxiety was great within me, your consolation brought me joy.

PSALM 94:19

It was getting late and the time for me to leave my friend's house
had come. She had agreed to support me in my business and
invited several friends over to join in the fun. But smiling and
holding conversations had become painful for me. Every few
minutes, I quietly excused myself to the restroom and silently
had a meltdown. The pounding and rumbling on my chest grew
stronger throughout the evening. When the party was over, I was
relieved to finally make my escape.

Cranking the car, my hands froze on the steering wheel. Somehow,
I had to get home to my family. Finally, I felt the Anxiety
Elephants retreat, so I turned the ignition and backed up. But
pulling onto the empty highway made me realize those elephants
were just hiding and waiting to give the knock-out blow. I had
to pull over. The anxiety became too great to for me to bear. The
only thing I could do was sit and wait until it passed.

Crushing blows from Anxiety Elephants pin you to the ground, they overpower you, and leave you lying like a rag doll in the aftermath. They overtake you and make you feel beat up and defeated. Anxiety does not wait for you to get ready to deal with its attack. It wants to be the superior force in your mind and heart.

I decided to look up the definition of the word "consolation" in today's verse. Merriam-Webster's Dictionary tells us it means: the act or an instance of consoling—comfort. So, our verse is telling us when the feeling of anxiety is great, God's comfort will bring us joy.

Notice the writer of this Psalm says, "When anxiety was great within me." He did not say "if." He is showing us anxious thoughts will come after us. Thoughts of sorrow, pain, worry, conflict, doubt, fear. The list could go on and on.

I totally get it. I know what it is like when Anxiety Elephants appear to overpower us. I know how it feels when they paralyze you and you can literally do nothing.

BUT—I also know the other side, something I desperately want you to know. I know what it is like to feel God's comfort and His loving arms wrapped around you. His great big bear hug brings your soul such delight when you turn into this loving embrace.

At times, I resisted this solace because I didn't think I deserved it. Thankfully, God does not give us what we deserve. He gives us what He longs for us to have, and that is communion with Him. Don't resist His comfort and joy today. He loves you. The satisfaction you will find in His care will beat back any Anxiety Elephant coming after you. Draw near to Him. Sit at His feet. Let Him give you what you don't deserve.

Action Step

Find a place where you can be alone for a few minutes. It will feel uncomfortable at first but be quiet and still. Ask God to help you feel His loving arms wrapped around you. Sit in that moment and let Him love you.

Prayer

Dear Heavenly Daddy, I want to feel your comfort and joy when anxiety seems great. Please let me feel your loving arms around me as I sit at your feet. Amen.

Journal Your Thoughts Below

_____

_____

_____

_____

_____

_____

_____

_____

_____

_____

_____

_____

_____

_____

_____

_____

_____

_____

_____

Day Twenty-Five

But now, this is what the Lord says…"Fear not,
for I have redeemed you; I have summoned you
by name; you are mine."

ISAIAH 43:1

I love the phrase *but now* in the Bible. It has always been a signal
for me to make a shift. Something new and different is about to
happen. Change is coming in an amazing way. Even as I type this,
I am sitting up in my chair with anticipation for what is coming
for you!

For so long, Anxiety Elephants have held you down. They have
bullied you, danced on you, trampled you, attacked you, and
belittled you. They have stolen your joy and robbed you of living
your life to the fullest. They have sucked the enthusiasm out of
you. They have controlled you.

Today, it all changes. No more living bound by their shackles
and chains. Anxiety Elephants are liars and they have no power
or authority over you or your life. As Deuteronomy 30:3 (MSG)

tells us, "God, your God, will restore everything you lost; he'll have compassion on you; he'll come back and pick up the pieces from all the places where you were scattered."

Your *but now* moment is happening. There is a transformation taking place even as you are reading this devotional. Your spirit is rising up as you realize God is telling you exactly who you are and what to do!

He is first telling you to *fear not.* You do not have to be afraid of Anxiety Elephants anymore. They may have convinced you for a while you are powerless against them, even hopeless. But redemption has happened for you by the work of your Heavenly Father, so this is not the case. His atonement is helping you overcome something as detrimental as anxiety.

Notice God's love in this passage. He has summoned us or called us by name. You are His. You belong to God. He has named you.

If you were to look up today's scripture in the Bible, you would find it goes on to tell us in verse two, "When we pass through the waters, He will be with us and the flames of the fire will not consume us." This means difficult times will not take you out. The Anxiety Elephants do not get to win.

Anxiety Elephants may have convinced you that you were about to burn in the flames, *but now*, God has shown you those flames cannot consume you.

Anxiety Elephants may have made you feel like you were going to drown under their pressure, *but now*, God has shown you He is carrying you through those waters and they will not overcome you.

Anxiety Elephants may have told you that you didn't matter, and no one cares, *but now,* you know you are important to your Abba Father and He calls you by name. You belong to Him.

Seize your *but now* moment today. Turn the page. Grab a hold of these truths. Yes, it is difficult but now you know the Anxiety Elephants do not win. You are not fighting for victory, *but now,* you are fighting *from* victory!

Action Step

Could you feel yourself rising up with hope as you read the verse for today? Did you feel a conversion in your thinking? I hope so. To keep walking in this *but now* moment, write down the changes you want to happen in your life, below. It may look something like this: I walk with my head hung low in shame, *but now*, I know God has redeemed me and restored me. I hide in fear because the Anxiety Elephants are so big, *but now*, I know they are not bigger than my God and He is fighting for me. I felt like anxiety stole my purpose from me, *but now*, I am taking it back! It's time to walk in your *but now* moment.

Prayer

Praise you Father, for my "but now" moment. Thank you for the shift. I am excited to walk in this step with you, Lord. Amen.

Journal Your Thoughts Below

_____

_____

_____

_____

_____

_____

_____

_____

_____

_____

_____

_____

_____

_____

_____

_____

_____

_____

_____

Day Twenty-Six

Behold, I am doing a new thing; now it springs
forth, do you not perceive it? I will make a way
in the wilderness and rivers in the desert.

ISAIAH 43:19

Yesterday, you had your *but now* moment. You turned the page on
your old way of thinking and living. Now, it is time to walk in the
new. And guess what? New is exciting, but new can be hard.

I would love to give you all warm fuzzies and make you think this
is going to be a cakewalk, but I would be doing you a disservice.
I am thrilled about the new happening for you, but it is going to
take some work. It is going to take walking through more emotional wilderness.

God made a way out of Egypt for the Israelites, out of the place
holding them in bondage and captivity for so long. And He has
a new place for you just as He did for them, but they had to go
through some tough terrain to get there. Many of them did not
handle this part of the journey very well, and they missed their

promised land as a result. I don't want you or I to miss out on what God has for us.

Continuing into the new, requires doing some new things on our end. This is not a one-way street where God puts in all the effort. We have to remember James 2:17 (paraphrased): "faith without works is dead."

To walk this out, we are going to have to put the work in. So, what does this new work look like?

If we want to experience a new and different way of living, we have to challenge ourselves in this new way of walking—stepping in faith. It requires changing what we are doing now. Whether we want to admit it or not, our old habits have opened the door for Anxiety Elephants to come in and harass us. If we are ready to destroy them, we must take a first step of faith.

Second, change what you do first thing in the morning. I have learned over the years that when I stop grabbing my phone to see what everyone is saying about my social media posts, or to see what everyone else is doing, and instead, grab my Bible to see what God is saying, I am more equipped to fight any anxiety trying to come my way. Opening His Word first thing will keep our focus on Him. By focusing on God, He can come and deal with the elephants better than what we can do on our own.

Next, changing what we think about can help us walk in a new way. If we are still thinking with our old pattern of thoughts, we will follow those thoughts back to Egypt, a place representing captivity.

To go to a new place, we have to shut the door to our thoughts of old. If you are still constantly thinking about how you aren't good enough, how you will never measure up, how God can never use you, or how Anxiety Elephants are taking everything from you, you can no longer stay there. Start giving thought to how God has truly created you for a purpose. Think about who He says you are and remind yourself you can do all things through Him (Philippians 4:13). Breaking old thought chains are difficult, but they can be shattered. Eventually, you will begin to believe and live them out.

Finally, have accountability in your life. We have discussed on previous days that when we are in isolation, we keep the door shut to everyone. Anxiety thrives in this environment. If no one is involved in our lives, they will never know what our struggle is, and we will never have to answer to anyone. This gives Anxiety Elephants the upper hand. However, when we let walls down and begin to share our struggles with people who can help us and hold us accountable, it gives us the upper hand. It keeps us focused on walking in a new pattern of faith, thinking, and living. Accountability is not meant to shame you. Accountability is there to grow you and stretch you into all God has created you to be.

It's time to walk in the new thing God has for you. Shut the door on old patterns and old ways of thinking. Let go of the door handle of your past and walk towards this new world. Open it with faith. Trust God to give you everything you need.

Action Step

Which step do you need to take today? Is it a step of faith to close the door on the old? Is it changing your thoughts or changing what you do first thing in the morning? Maybe you need to go a little further and create accountability in your life. Write down which step you are going to take today as you begin walking in a NEW thing.

Prayer

Lord, I know I need to make some changes and I need help. Show me how I can transform my thoughts and add accountability to my life. I want to walk in this new way You desire for me, and I know these steps will be an important part. Amen.

Journal Your Thoughts Below

_____

_____

_____

_____

_____

_____

_____

_____

_____

_____

_____

_____

_____

_____

_____

_____

_____

_____

_____

_____

Day Twenty-Seven

About midnight Paul and Silas were praying and singing hymns to God, and the prisoners were listening to them, and suddenly there was a great earthquake, so that the foundations of the prison were shaken. And immediately all the doors were opened, and everyone's bonds were unfastened.

ACTS 16:25-26

One of my favorite things to do is lead worship music with my husband at church. We were worship leaders when the Anxiety Elephants decided to pick on me. I was getting to serve the Lord, something I love, and then the rug was completely pulled out from under me. I went from loving to sing and worship God to being scared into silence.

Anxiety Elephants (a weapon of Satan), know the power of worship. Our enemy is not ill-equipped. Before his fall, he was in Heaven with God. Along with us, Satan was created to worship God (Colossians 1:15-16). He knows worship was a command given throughout the Bible. We see it in the Old Testament when David offers up a song of thanksgiving because the ark of the covenant had been returned—commanding the Israelites to sing to the Lord and proclaim His salvation day after day (1 Chronicles 16:23-31). In the New Testament, we are called to let our lives be an example of worship—a sacrifice of praise every day not conforming to the ways of the world (Romans 12:1-2). Our adversary attacks our thoughts to get the weapon of worship out of our hands. He knows praise brings breakthrough, walls fall, victories in battle take place, and the salvation of others can result.

In the passage immediately prior to today's scripture, we find these two Christ-followers, Paul and Silas, going to a place of prayer. A slave girl who is possessed by a demon, follows—and nags them. Paul is annoyed and finally casts out the demon. It makes her owners mad. They have Paul and Silas beaten and thrown into jail. These disciples simply want to pray and seek the Lord, but the enemy is not going to let them worship that easily. He doesn't let any of us serve God without a fight. But like Paul and Silas, when we persist, our bonds ultimately fall away, too.

Have you tried to tell Anxiety Elephants to leave you alone, only to have the enemy attack harder? Have you ever felt like you were thrown into a prison? Paul and Silas were tossed into a dark place, much like the darkness we experience when anxiety casts a shadow over our lives. The disciples could have sat in fear and let the darkness silence them, but instead, they chose to pray and sing to the Lord. This shook the walls of their cell and knocked them down—and the walls of everyone around them collapsed, as well.

When Paul and Silas sat in the dungeon praising and worshiping

God, they knew they could trust Him in the cell. I can only speculate that they were hurting and sore, but their focus was on WHO had more power than the bars that imprisoned them. If Anxiety Elephants have beaten you up pretty good, you may feel fairly bruised yourself. But God is more powerful than anything Anxiety Elephants may have thrown at you.

Because Paul and Silas were in this prison, God was able to use them to save the guard. Prison was probably the last place they wanted to be, and I am sure getting beaten up was not on their top ten list of things to do while traveling. Even so, God was able to use the pain and their chains to set others free.

God is ready to knock down the walls the Anxiety Elephants have put you behind. He is ready to break off the chains. When you open your mouth in faith and worship the King of Kings, the earth will move, and your enemy will shake, when you sing in spite of your circumstances.

Action Step

When you find Anxiety Elephants charging towards you, choose to worship. It will be a choice—it will not come naturally. Remember, this is a powerful weapon in your arsenal. God will hear you. The walls will crumble. Victory will come. Today, stand firm and worship.

Prayer

I worship You, Almighty God. I praise You, the Creator of this Universe and thank you for your desire to have a relationship with me. Thank You for loving me the way You do. Help my mind to stay on You today. I love You. Amen.

Journal Your Thoughts Below

_____

_____

_____

_____

_____

_____

_____

_____

_____

_____

_____

_____

_____

_____

_____

_____

_____

_____

Day Twenty-Eight

And we know that for those who love God all
things work together for good, for those who
are called according to his purpose.

ROMANS 8:28

Facing Anxiety Elephants daily can make it hard for you to
imagine that God could or would use your struggles for good. In
fact, there may be days when you think your life should be over,
because the mental battle is so fierce. Sometimes, anxiety even
brings friends along to terrorize you: depression, anger, doubt,
confusion, helplessness, etc. They fight sneaky and dirty. Focused
on them, you can see nothing good around you.

That's when you have to change where you are looking. When
you put all your attention on Anxiety Elephants and company,
your vision becomes blurred. Anxiety appears bigger than what
it really is. It looks as though it is larger than life and too big for
God to handle.

Instead of focusing on your emotions though, look up to your

Defender. There is nothing too big for God to defeat. Anxiety Elephants may have snuck up on you, but they never caught Him off guard. Turn to Him when they show up. Put your eyes on the victory and not on the pain and the battle. He will overcome on your behalf.

Once you stop trying to fight on your own and let God do His thing, you become stronger and more confident. You can come out from under those elephant's feet. You will exchange positions and stand on your attacker's back.

This allows us to learn and rely on the Lord and His strength. It teaches us to stop looking at the problem and instead look at the Problem Solver.

When we learn how to use the tools God has given us to fight Anxiety Elephants off, we can start helping others. There was a time I couldn't imagine writing devotionals on overcoming anxiety. I could not see the possibility when I was in the middle of my struggles. But I am on the other side of the battle now, and I realize God didn't just teach me how to overcome for my sake alone. He helped me so I could help others. He is helping you, so you too, can help others.

The Lord may use you to support a co-worker who has no one else to confide in about their anxiety. He may use you in a mom's group to show other women they are not crazy even if their thoughts make them feel that way. God may use you to help others see that they can laugh in the face of anxiety and help them trust it does not get to win. He may even use you to show your battle to someone, and in turn, give them the courage to no longer hide their own struggle. When we reveal the truth, healing can begin.

I don't know how God is going to put this to work for good in your life, but I do know this—give Him a chance, and He will.

Action Step

By changing your perspective on anxiety today, it could help someone else. Write down how you have seen God already use your situation for good, and any future way you hope to see Him use your battle to add value to others.

Prayer

Thank You Father, for using anxiety for good in my life. Thank you for being the Great Defender on my behalf. Amen.

Journal Your Thoughts Below

_____

_____

_____

_____

_____

_____

_____

_____

_____

_____

_____

_____

_____

_____

_____

_____

_____

_____

_____

_____

Day Twenty-Nine

As each has received a gift, use it to serve one
another, as good stewards of God's varied grace:

1 PETER 4:10

*"Me? I have gifts to use to help other people? How in the world can
I help others after all the struggles I have been through? Why would
God ever trust someone like me to go and help someone else? If I tell
them I have dealt with anxiety, will they turn away and not listen?
Can I really go out there and be all God's Word says I am? Am I ready
for this?"*

Do you find yourself asking these questions?

Nearing the end of this devotional, there are likely days you are
ready to go conquer the world, and then there are days you think
you have made zero progress. The mind can prove a very tricky
place.

Cling to this good news: God's Word is true. It is the same yesterday, today, and forever. Just as God's Word was true for the

disciples and those living hundreds of years before us, it is true for you and me. It will be true for the generations who come after us.

We each have received a gift. Those gifts will shine brightest through the broken places of our lives. Where God heals us, we experience His love, grace, mercy and forgiveness. We can serve others best by understanding where brokenness can take a person, and in turn, where God can take the person through it.

I must admit, I used to be one of those people who didn't think anxiety, or any mental health issues, were real. I believed they constituted a bunch of baloney claimed by people who were selfish, lazy, or who just felt sorry for themselves. I never gave anxiety-ridden people compassion. I never talked to them with the love of Jesus.

After having Anxiety Elephants nearly take me out, I began to truly understand on some level, what others were experiencing. I learned how suffocating anxiety could be. I felt the effects of it choking the life out of me. Even though I wanted to be out from under the grip of anxiety, I couldn't do it alone.

Because of the broken areas anxiety brought about in my life, I experienced healing I didn't realize I needed, when Jesus began to breathe redemption into those places. I began to feel compassion the way Jesus had compassion. He gave me a gift of hope and restoration. I wanted those who battle Anxiety Elephants to know the gifts available to them. I had to share what I'd learned. People attacked by anxiety need to know what is available for them—including you.

Open your gift. God has given you a story. He didn't give this to you for you to keep to yourself. He gave it to you because there is someone out there who needs to hear from you. They too, may think they are the only ones who get trampled on by Anxiety Elephants. They may believe this is the way life is meant to be. There are people waiting on you to share your gift with them.

Walk in the gift of grace God has given you. He will be with you. He will give you the words and gentleness you need to share with those He places in your path. It could be one or it could be thousands—the number doesn't matter. It's most important we continue to share what God has taught us and spread a message of hope and redemption around the world.

Action Step

Share your gift—story. Write it here first to help you. Share it with your accountability partner if you need extra courage. Someone out there is waiting to hear what God's grace, hope, and redemption can do for them.

Prayer

Give me courage to share my story, Lord. Thank You for giving me hope. Help me to share it with others who are searching. Amen.

Journal Your Thoughts Below

Day Thirty

They triumphed over him by the blood of the
Lamb and the word of their testimony.

REVELATION 12:11A

Sitting in a cozy living room along with several women, it was my
turn to share. This time I felt something different. Hope was rising
inside of me and would not allow me to push it back down. But I
didn't want to share this intimate part of my story, yet. *Surely God,
it is too soon*, I thought. *Please tell me I get more time than this to
enjoy my newfound freedom from the nasty Anxiety Elephants?*

Tell them, I felt the Holy Spirit whisper. So, I did. In the midst
of nerves wound tight like a rubber band, I told them. I shared
not just the good, but also the bad and the darkness from the
past few months of my life. Tears soaked the floor beneath me. I
looked up and saw something I didn't expect. I saw others with
puddles that had fallen in front of them. They were experiencing
similar emotions as me. On that day, hope found them. A story
of overcoming the ugly side of anxiety spoke freedom into their

cold, bound souls. My story helped others see that victory could happen for them, too.

Will you ever overcome your Anxiety Elephants? The answer is: YES, you will! Just know it takes time. God's healing needs to infiltrate the places Anxiety Elephants have made camp in for so long. Persisting, so you can prevail against the enemy is key to walking the path towards victory.

Today's scripture tells us how to overcome: By the blood of the Lamb and the word of our testimony.

Jesus did His part. He shed every drop of His blood on the cross for you and me. He did this out of obedience to His Father and His love for us. Now, it's your turn. There is someone out there who needs to hear about your struggle with anxiety. They need to hear you are overcoming, and how you are conquering anxiety. They need hope.

What I am challenging you to do is to help someone else. Share your testimony. Know that your puddle of tears will give them freedom to finally release the broken pieces they have carried for so long. You offer healing. If you see a friend struggling, let her know you understand and care. If you see someone post on social media, send a message of encouragement.

Think about it like this—where would you be if no one was willing to help and share with you? You can do this. God will help you. Now is your time to overcome.

Action Step

Look for one person you can share your testimony with—this goes beyond telling your story. This is about telling your truth and sharing the depth of how God has brought you healing. Ask God to give you the words others need to hear.

Prayer

Thank you Jesus, for your blood, shed for me. Thank you that we can overcome, because of your sacrifice and power. Thank you for doing your part willingly for me. Help me do my part to share the testimony you have given me. Amen.

Journal Your Thoughts Below

_____

_____

_____

_____

_____

_____

_____

_____

_____

_____

_____

_____

_____

_____

_____

_____

_____

_____

Day Thirty-One

Therefore, there is now no condemnation for those who are in Christ Jesus.

ROMANS 8:1

The directive has been somewhat similar over these thirty-one days. As each page turned, you read one particular message at least once—you are not alone. God hears you, there is hope, and Anxiety Elephants can be defeated. You read multiple times about the importance of seeking help, journaling, accountability, faith, prayer and worship.

Why would I include a similar message over and over?

Because reminders are needed! The Anxiety Elephants have pushed their agenda into your mind and soul longer than you may want to admit. Their message is one of constant shame and repetitive condemnation. If they can keep you down, they know you will not become everything God wants you to be. I'm here to ensure they fail.

If they keep reciting the same message of fear, shame, and judgment, why do we think we need to stop listening to the echoes of hope on a regular basis? Why do we think we only need to hear once that there is no condemnation in Christ Jesus?

Zig Ziglar said it best, "People often say motivation doesn't last. Well, neither does bathing, that's why we recommend it daily."

I love this statement! We take baths daily to stay clean. We brush our teeth every day to keep our teeth strong and prevent stinky breath. If we do these tasks daily to help our body, shouldn't we also have daily habits that will cleanse our minds and souls?

It is so important on your quest to destroy Anxiety Elephants that you continually remind yourself that Jesus has never condemned or shamed you. He doesn't look at you differently because of your struggle. He doesn't close His arms off to you. Instead, He opens His arms wide to say, "Come. I am right here, waiting."

When you feel accusations come at you, and you will, you need to know you no longer have to receive them. You can push back and let Anxiety Elephants know they no longer get to have space in your head. You are now equipped with scripture, tools, and weapons to silence the ridicule and disapproval from their voices.

Get up and refresh your memory every day on who God has called you and what He has gifted you to do that no one else can. Continue to open the Bible and spend time in His Word, even when the days seem easy. You won't always go through a battle, but you always need to be prepared for one. That's how Anxiety Elephants got in to begin with—they caught us off guard.

Choose the messages you allow into your mind, and the ones you push out. You will have to plant seeds of life and faith where seeds of doubt and fear once lived. Without exception, remember God has His job under control.

You are prepared.

You are ready.

You are equipped.

Now, keep stomping out Anxiety Elephants. They are no match for God's children.

Action Step

This is the last day. What are some of your big takeaways? Do you feel more prepared to crush Anxiety Elephants? Has your faith strengthened? Do you feel encouraged to make changes so you can see transformation in your life? Write out a purpose statement below. As you close this devotional, what do you want to see happen? How do you want God to use you? How do you want to grow? Write it out, sign, then date it, and surrender your commitment to the Lord. Remember, you are not alone and nothing in your life will be wasted. He is about to do a new thing in you and through you!

Prayer

Thank you Father, for all the things I have learned and the weapons you have given me to stomp out Anxiety Elephants every day. Help me put these resources to use and stand strong. Hallelujah! Amen!

Journal Your Thoughts Below

_____

_____

_____

_____

_____

_____

_____

_____

_____

_____

_____

_____

_____

_____

_____

_____

_____

_____

Conclusion

Well, you made it! For some of you, you completed this thirty-one day devotional early. Others did it in the thirty-one day span. There are some of you, like me, who take a bit longer. All these ways are just fine, and you want to know why? Because you finished the book. You took the time to read, and hopefully apply, some things you learned. That is a triumph!

I hope you are now able to identify your triggers and know what to do when and if Anxiety Elephants come. I hope you found some scriptures that spoke directly to your heart and helped you recall God's truth, so you are ready when Anxiety Elephants try to knock you down. I hope you held on to action steps you can apply to your life when Anxiety Elephants try a sneak attack. I hope you journaled and wrote down feelings you have locked inside for many years.

Freedom. I hope you found freedom.

Am I completely free from Anxiety Elephants? I would really love to tell you yes, but the truth is, I'm not. I still have my days—my moments where Anxiety Elephants sneak up on me.

But it doesn't happen as often anymore. The tools, scriptures, and action steps I shared with you are things I still use on a regular basis. By being prepared, I am now stronger than the Anxiety Elephants. This will be true for you as well. The more you put these suggestions into practice, the more strength you will have to stand against an attack.

God has equipped you with everything you need for battle. Stand strong and bear in mind you are not fighting alone. We are waging war next to each other, for each other, and with each other. You've got this. Keep stomping, my friend!

About the Author

Caris Snider

Caris Snider is a Christian Communicator who shares the hope of God through traveling to speak, leading worship, and writing. Her passion for the Lord comes forth as she shares from her experiences of overcoming depression, anxiety, fear, and shame. Caris desires to help women of all generations to see their value and worth through the eyes of the Lord. It is important to her to give a voice to the voiceless and help those who feel alone. Caris wants everyone to find the freedom to go after their purpose and calling on their lives because no one else can accomplish what God created them to do. To contact Caris about her ministry and the opportunity to partner with you, go to: carissnider.com.

Stay Connected!

Instagram	@carissnider
Facebook	@carissnider
YouTube	@carissnider